FIFTY WAYS TO TEACH WRITING

Tips for ESL/EFL Teachers

MAGGIE SOKOLIK

50 Ways to Teach Writing: Tips for ESL/EFL Teachers, 2nd Edition

Copyright © 2012; 2020 by Wayzgoose Press

All rights reserved. No part of this publication may be reproduced, stored in or introduced into a retrieval system, or transmitted, in any form, or by any means (electronic, mechanical, photocopying, recording, or otherwise) without the prior written permission of the copyright owner.

Edited by Dorothy E. Zemach. Cover design by DJ Rogers.

Published in the United States by Wayzgoose Press.

CONTENTS

How to Use This Book   v
Introduction   vii

PART I
PREWRITING, PLANNING, AND STRATEGIES

1. Brainstorm/Make a List   3
2. Mind Map   5
3. Reconstruct an Outline   7
4. Cubing   9
5. Focused Freewrite   11
6. Inventory of Knowledge   13
7. Idea Analysis   15
8. Word Association   17
9. Word Storm   19
10. Write from a Model   21
11. Interviews   25
12. Conduct a Poll   27
13. Summarize Data   29
14. Keep a Reading Journal   33
15. Use a Quotation   35
16. Physical Observation   37
17. Classroom Strategies   39

PART II
WRITING TOPICS AND STRATEGIES

18. Use a Photograph   43
19. Chain Paragraph   45
20. Finish the Story   49
21. "Dear Abby"   51
22. Map Stories   53
23. Dicto-Comp   55
24. Write Instructions   57

25. Comparison for Recommendation	59
26. Write Two Letters	61
27. Index Card Summaries	63
28. Movie and Book Reviews	65
29. Blank Comics	67
30. Advertisement	71
31. What/Who am I?	73
32. Thesis Statements	75
33. Crazy Paragraph	79
34. Write a Proper Email	81
35. Model Paragraphs	83
36. Using Transitions	85
37. Paraphrase	87
38. Culture Wiki	89
39. Create a Cloze	91
40. Sentence Completions	95

PART III
EDITING AND REVISING

41. Writer's Memo	99
42. Writing on the Wall	101
43. Reverse Outlining	103
44. Keep an Error Journal	105
45. Search and Replace	107
46. Error Correction in Context	109
47. Demonstrate Revision	111
48. Prepare for Peer Reading and Review	113
49. Changing Nouns to Verbs	117
50. Listen to Your Writing	119
Bonus Tip: Story Box	121

HOW TO USE THIS BOOK

Most teachers use a textbook in class, which provides both instruction and practice—but, often, not enough practice. Students need to practice again and again, and in different ways, not just to keep their interest but to both learn and remember.

This book gives you ideas to help your students practice writing in English. It can be used with any textbook, or without any textbook at all. It tells you how to adapt and extend exercises; it gives you prewriting, topics, and revision activities that can be added to any class.

Not every idea will work for every student or for every class. That's why there are fifty. We feel sure that many of the ideas presented here will bring you results if you try them sincerely and practice them regularly.

Here is a suggested method for using this book:

1. Read through all of the fifty tips without stopping.
2. Read through the tips again. Choose five or six that

you think might work for your class. Decide when you will try them.
3. Choose different types of ideas: Some that can be done independently, and some that work along with your textbook; some that focus on creative writing, and some that focus on specific skills.
4. Each time you use one of the ways, make a note about how well it worked for you and why. Remember that most of the tips will work best if you use them several times (or even make them a habit). Don't try a tip only once and decide it's not good for your students. Give the tips you try at least a few chances.
5. Every few weeks, read through the tips again, and choose some new ones. Discontinue using any methods that are not working for you and your students.

Finally, consider trying some of the other books in our *Fifty Ways to Teach* series. No one skill in English is really separate from the others. Speaking, listening, reading, writing, vocabulary, and grammar are all connected. Students who improve in one area will almost always improve in other areas, too. The series also includes special volumes for teaching young learners, teenagers, using technology in the classroom, and professional development.

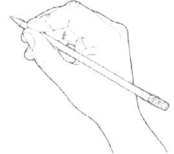

INTRODUCTION

This book is for teachers who are new to working with English language learners, new to teaching writing, or are simply looking for more creative and engaging writing activities for their English classes. This isn't a presentation of research and pedagogy, but a list of writing activities and tips for making these activities more effective. Many of the ideas are based on a process approach to writing—that is, it looks at writing as a system of planning, drafting, and revision.

Of course, not all these tips may work for your class exactly as written. It is always beneficial to consider an idea and think about how you could adapt it to your own context. When you read a tip, think about how you could change it to fit your students' ages, levels, cultural backgrounds, and interests.

You might also try completing the task described in the tip yourself. This will help you anticipate questions your students might have, or know in advance how long it might take for them to complete it. Of course, you should feel free to adapt the activities in any way you like.

INTRODUCTION

This book is divided into three categories, which represent the stages of process writing:

1. Pre-writing and planning
2. Writing topics and strategies
3. Editing and revising

The process approach, however, is not linear; students might plan, write, rewrite, and re-plan and rewrite recursively, or in any order, as shown in the figure below.

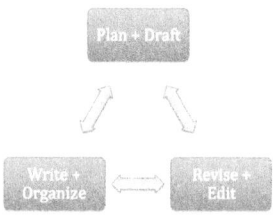

The Process Approach

One piece of advice: As you plan your writing assignments, think about your *last assignment first*. That is, what is the final assignment that your students will be asked to complete? What assignments do they need to do along the way to finish that assignment successfully? Thinking about how to plan and build your assignments will help your students achieve success; it will help you determine which of the tips will be most useful for your class.

Finally, whether you are using this book as part of a writing course, or you are using writing as part of a multi-skills course, you should find something of use here. If you have ideas or amendments to the tips here, please send them to us at editor@wayzgoosepress.com for consideration in future editions.

You can find photocopiable pages in the paper version of this book, or PDFs of worksheets to use with some of the tips at: anglofile.com/50ways/. You are free to photocopy and distribute these worksheets to your students.

❧ 1 ☙
PREWRITING, PLANNING, AND STRATEGIES

Prewriting, planning, and developing strategies are important steps in the writing process. Students will find it easier to complete a writing assignment if they've spent some time brainstorming, taking notes, and working together to think about assignments before they begin any formal writing.

Read through these possibilities for prewriting or planning activities. Choose one or two to use before you give your next writing assignment.

Remember to keep notes on what goes well and what needs improvement, so the next time you use a tip, you are ready to present it in an even better way.

I
BRAINSTORM/MAKE A LIST

Brainstorming is a good activity for students who need to generate ideas for writing.

Ask students to consider a particular topic you've given them (or that they have created themselves). Then, they should list everything they want to say about it. Hierarchy is not important here—the idea is to get down as many ideas as possible. Students can organize, create hierarchies, or outlines, after they create their lists.

EXAMPLE

Topic: Healthy lifestyle

- fruit
- vegetables
- healthy protein
- whole grains
- drinking water

- exercise
- sleep

2
MIND MAP

Mind maps appeal to students who like drawing and visual representations of their ideas. They are a useful visual for helping to brainstorm and organize ideas.

Students begin by writing a key word or idea in the center of a page, and drawing a circle around it.

Next, they think of other words or phrases that are connected to that key word. They then write the associated ideas and words around the central circle, and draw lines or arrows from the main idea to show connections.

These maps can eventually be turned into outlines or plans for an essay or short writing assignment.

EXAMPLE

The following figure shows a mind map based on the concept *entertainment* and its related ideas.

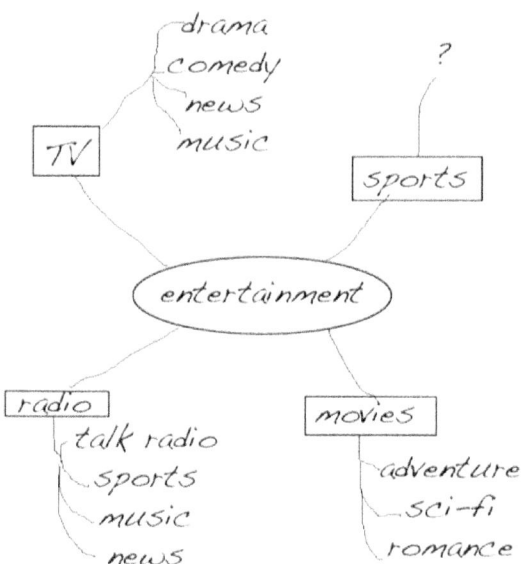

A sample mind map

3
RECONSTRUCT AN OUTLINE

For this activity, students work in pairs to improve the organization of their outlines and essay ideas.

Each student should write an outline—without numbers or letters—for an essay or story they are working on (this should be done on paper). Next, they cut their outline into strips, each strip being one part of the outline.

In their pairs, students should exchange their outlines, and try to put each other's outlines back in the intended order.

They should discuss the results, especially the places where they were confused in putting the outline back in order.

CUBING

This activity asks students to consider a topic or writing prompt from six different angles (think of the six faces of a cube).

Write the topic on the board or hand it out on a sheet of paper. Ask students to divide a blank sheet of paper into six sections, and label the sections: *who*, *what*, *when*, *why*, *where*, and *how*.

If you like, you can even construct your own version of a question cube out of paper or cardboard. This isn't necessary, but most students enjoy being able to hold and look at the cubes. Create several and let students pass them around. Here are some simple instructions with pictures:

https://www.wikihow.com/Fold-an-Origami-Cube

Ask students to write without stopping for two minutes on each aspect of the topic. They can use these notes to develop the topic into an essay or more complete assignment.

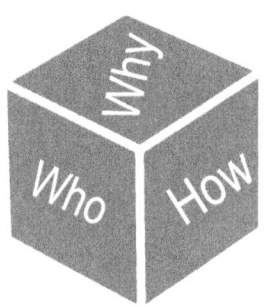

Example of a question cube

FOCUSED FREEWRITE

This activity helps develop writing fluency and confidence in getting started.

Set a time limit, and have students write *without stopping* to erase or correct themselves for that period of time. Tell hem not to worry about grammar, spelling, punctuation, or vocabulary. The purpose is to write without inhibition.

Give them a topic to write about, perhaps something related to a reading or other assignment they are working on.

Note: Focused freewrites should not be corrected, graded or assessed; the purpose is to encourage students to write without inhibition. You may want to give students credit for completing the exercise, but if you tell them not to worry about grammar or punctuation, then it isn't fair to grade the work.

VARIATIONS

1. Have a student choose a topic for the day and write it on the board for the class.
2. Put a quote of the day on the board and have students write about it. You can find many good quotations at bartleby.com/quotations/.

6
INVENTORY OF KNOWLEDGE

This activity helps students use the collective knowledge of a group to generate writing ideas about particular topics.

Students work in groups of three or four. You can assign them a specific topic for their assignment, or have them choose one of their own in their groups.

After a topic is chosen or assigned, they should discuss and write down everything they know about the topic. They will use this shared knowledge as information for their writing assignment.

EXAMPLE

Topic: Science Fiction

- a type of imaginative literature
- futuristic concepts
- science and technology
- time travel

- parallel universes
- robots
- cyber-humans
- space exploration
- extraterrestrial life (ET)

7
IDEA ANALYSIS

This activity helps students to think critically about a topic, and think about it in more nuanced and sophisticated ways.

Ask students to choose a concept or topic to write about, or give them a topic. Have them write this topic at the top of their papers.

Next, they should explain the meaning of or define the idea in one or two sentences, and give a relevant example. As the final step, they should evaluate the concept by listing its pros and cons, or positive and negative aspects. They can then use this information to build an essay on the topic.

EXAMPLE

Topic: The benefit of electric cars

Explanation: This topic is asking for the positive aspects of cars that do not use gasoline to operate. An example of this would be using cars that you can plug into your electricity at home.

Positive aspects: lower costs, cheaper maintenance, in some places, there are tax advantages, etc.

Negative aspects: shorter range (you can't drive very far with some electric cars), increased electricity bills, battery replacement is expensive, etc.

8
WORD ASSOCIATION

This activity helps students use vocabulary to expand their thinking about writing topics.

To help students explore possible topics, write four or five keywords on the board. Ask students to list these keywords on a sheet of paper. Then, next to each keyword, they should write as many related words as possible.

Finally, they choose the one keyword that generated the most interesting associations in order to develop their essay or assignment.

EXAMPLE

Keywords: travel, languages, cultures, art

travel: trains, planes, automobiles, boats, adventure, excitement, etc.

languages: learning, dictionaries, translation, grammar, learning, nouns, etc.

9
WORD STORM

This activity helps students focus on vocabulary development in their writing.

Bring an entire print newspaper to class and pass it around, instructing students to pull out a page that has an article of interest to them.

Ask them to read the article, circling or highlighting **all** the words they don't know.

Next, have them write all their circled words on the board. The board should gradually fill up with words.

Finally, ask students to identify five (or ten, or whatever number you think suitable) words that they do not know and that interest them.

Their follow-up work is to look up the words, write out their definitions, write original sentences using the words, and present one or more of their words to the class.

Note: It may be helpful for you or a student to take a photo of the board after it is filled with words. This will provide a vocabulary list to work on for as long as you want.

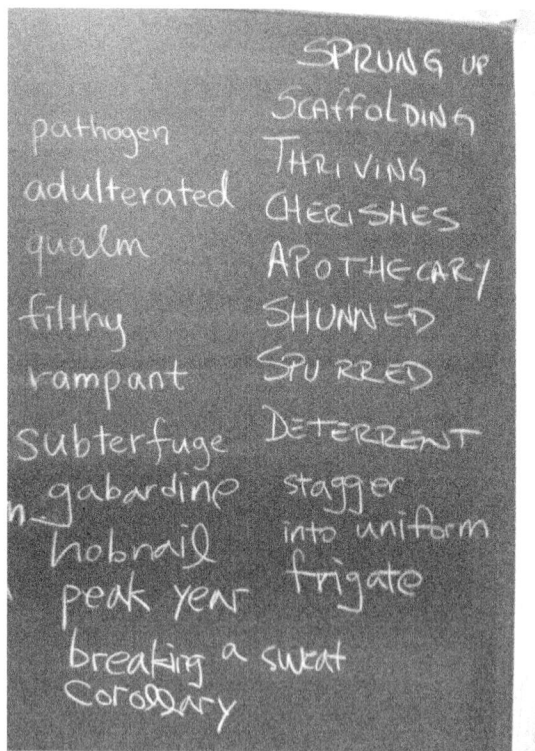

VARIATION

Have students write their words on the board without talking about the article. Ask students to guess from the vocabulary list what the article is about.

10
WRITE FROM A MODEL

Students can learn a lot about structure, vocabulary choice, and grammar by imitating a writing model.

Find an interesting or distinctive short piece of writing for students to imitate. Spend time in class going over the parts of the model, and drawing attention to important parts or elements of the original.

EXAMPLE

Here is an example you can use, written by the American writer Mark Twain. Ask the students to read the story carefully first, to ensure they understand it. Then, have them try to write a model, using the cloze activity that follows. They should consult the original story during this activity.

The River and Its History

by Mark Twain

The Mississippi is well worth reading about. It is not a commonplace river, but on the contrary is in all ways remarkable. Considering the Missouri its main branch, it is the longest river in the world—four thousand three hundred miles. It seems safe to say that it is also the crookedest river in the world, since in one part of its journey it uses up one thousand three hundred miles to cover the same ground that the crow would fly over in six hundred and seventy-five. It discharges three times as much water as the St. Lawrence, twenty-five times as much as the Rhine, and three hundred and thirty-eight times as much as the Thames. No other river has so vast a drainage-basin: it draws its water supply from twenty-eight States and Territories; from Delaware, on the Atlantic seaboard, and from all the country between that and Idaho on the Pacific slope—a spread of forty-five degrees of longitude. The Mississippi receives and carries to the Gulf water from fifty-four subordinate rivers that are navigable by steamboats, and from some hundreds that are navigable by flats and keels. The area of its drainage-basin is as great as the combined areas of England, Wales, Scotland, Ireland, France, Spain, Portugal, Germany, Austria, Italy, and Turkey; and almost all this wide region is fertile; the Mississippi valley, proper, is exceptionally so.

Instructions to the Students

Write a paragraph about another river you know, using Mark Twain's paragraph as an example. Use the cloze paragraph below to help you. Write in words or ideas that are correct for the river you choose.

Title: _____
by _____

The _____ (river name) _____. It is not a _____ river, _____. Considering the _____, it is the _____ river in _____ — _____. It seems safe to say that it is also the _____ river in _____, since in one part of its journey it uses up _____. It _____ as much water as _____. No other river has _____. _____ receives and carries to the _____ from _____ rivers that are _____. The area of its _____ is _____; and almost all this region is _____.

11
INTERVIEWS

Interviews are activities that combine listening, speaking, and writing skills. They also are typically a high-interest activity for students.

Conducting an interview is an interesting way to get information about a person's past job, habits, etc. Ask students to think of someone they would like to interview, such as a family member, a friend, or a teacher.

The first step is to write questions to ask the interviewee. You should check the questions to be sure they are clear and appropriate.

To record the details of the interview, students should either take notes or get the interviewee's permission to be recorded.

Afterwards, the students write up what they learned in the interview in narrative form.

VARIATION

For more advanced students, require that they use both direct and indirect quotations from their interviews in their writing.

CONDUCT A POLL

This is a group or pair activity that encourages original research and collaborative writing.

In pairs or small groups, students choose a characteristic that they want to know about a group of people, such as favorite television shows, information about educational achievement, or opinions about a current fashion or trend.

In their groups, students write 5-10 questions to use in their polls. You should check the questions to be sure they are clear and appropriate.

The students then conduct their polls face-to-face, by email, or by setting up an internet poll using a site such as Google Forms (only if they know how, or if you can teach them how).

As a group, they should write up their results, including any charts, images, or graphs if appropriate.

13
SUMMARIZE DATA

Lots of jobs and classes require summarizing data. This activity will help students with the vocabulary and structures to describe a data set.

Find a chart or table with data that might be interesting to your students, for example, the world's most populous cities, the most watched internet videos for the week, the number of bananas eaten nationally in a year in certain countries.

Project the data or give students a copy and ask them to write a paragraph or two (depending on how much data there is) that describes the data in an organized way.

Review target language and key phrases in advance, such as *An overwhelming majority, nearly half, three times as many, only a small percentage of.*

EXAMPLE

Here are two data sets you might use.

The 10 Most Populous Cities in the World

1. Shanghai, China (Population: 24,153,000)
2. Beijing, China (Population: 18,590,000)
3. Karachi, Pakistan (Population: 18,000,000)
4. Istanbul, Turkey (Population: 14,657,000)
5. Dhaka, Bangladesh (Population: 14,543,000)
6. Tokyo, Japan (Population: 13,617,000)
7. Moscow, Russia (Population: 13,197,596)
8. Manila, Philippines (Population: 12,877,000)
9. Tianjin, China (Population: 12,784,000)
10. Mumbai, India (Population: 12,400,00)

The Ten Most Popular Types of Fruit in the World

1. Tomatoes
2. Bananas
3. Watermelons
4. Apples
5. Grapefruit
6. Grapes
7. Oranges
8. Mangoes
9. Plantains
10. Tangerines

VARIATION

Rather than just describe and compare the data in one of these lists, ask students to react to it. You might ask them:

- *What surprises you about the world's most populous cities?*
- *Are there any types of fruit listed don't you like? Why?*
- etc.

14
KEEP A READING JOURNAL

This activity helps students connect reading and writing.

If reading is part of your class, ask students to keep a journal in which they respond to the reading in writing. Have them think about holding a conversation with the author, and ask questions of the text and author.

It may be helpful to start by giving them questions to answer in their journals.

For example:

- *Did you enjoy this reading? Why or why not?*
- *What did you learn from this reading?*
- *What else would you like to know?*
- *What would you like to ask the author?*

15
USE A QUOTATION

For students who have academic interests, learning to respond to and use quotations from reading is an important skill.

Ask students to write a paragraph explaining or responding to a quotation, using the quotation itself in the paragraph.

Have them use proper quotation formatting, including punctuation. They should include the name of the author of the quotation.

Some quotations can be found here: bartleby.com/quotations.

EXAMPLE

Shakespeare once wrote, "A rose by any other name...."

VARIATION

After students have written their direct quotation, have them change it into indirect speech (e.g., *Shakespeare wrote that a rose by another name...*).

16
PHYSICAL OBSERVATION

This activity asks students to observe carefully and write a paragraph about a location. It helps them to develop their skills in description and using descriptive vocabulary.

Ask students to think about any location of their choice. The goal is to practice using all their senses when writing.

Ask them to write a paragraph about the place they thought about: specifically, what they see, hear, smell, feel, and taste in that place.

VARIATION

Before this activity, have students do a pre-writing activity in which they work in groups to brainstorm as many words as possible relating to the different senses.

17
CLASSROOM STRATEGIES

In this activity, students use their collective experience to improve their writing practices.

Working in groups of three or four, students discuss and list all their strategies for starting a writing assignment.

Each group shares their strategies by writing them on large pieces of paper taped on the wall, written on the board, or by reading them for other students to take notes.

If students have a difficult time getting started, give them a couple of examples of strategies, such as:

- write an outline
- gather all the necessary materials together
- relax and meditate

❦ II ❦
WRITING TOPICS AND STRATEGIES

One of the biggest problems students confront is how to find something worthwhile to write about.

This section presents several topics you might use with students to help them begin writing. It also gives a number of strategies, or ways to encourage writing that may not focus on a specific topic.

Read through the ideas here and choose a topic or strategy that you think will work with your students. Again, keep records of how well each strategy works.

18
USE A PHOTOGRAPH

This activity uses visuals to encourage writing, especially with a focus on verb tense.

Show an interesting photograph using a projector, or bring one from a magazine or whatever resource is available to you. Ask students to write about what is happening in the photograph.

Grammar point: This activity focuses on using the present progressive. A good way to remind students that this is the required grammatical form is to ask: *What is happening in this picture?*

VARIATIONS

To focus on other verb tenses, here are two variations for this activity.

1. Ask the students to imagine and write about what happened just before the photograph was taken. This activity will focus on the simple past or past progressive tenses.

2. Ask them to imagine and write about what will happen next. This asks students to use the future aspect, especially the forms "will + infinitive" or "is/are going to + infinitive."

EXAMPLES

Present progressive: A flock of birds **is flying** near a large tree.

Past progressive: A flock of birds **was sitting** in a large tree.

Future aspect: A flock of birds **will fly** over the field and disappear from sight.

19
CHAIN PARAGRAPH

This is a fun activity that also helps students understand the ordering of information in a paragraph.

Students work in groups of four or five. Each student starts with a blank piece of paper.

Ask them to write a beginning or topic sentence. This topic sentence can be anything they want, or you might want to suggest that it be about something you're doing in class.

When they've written their first sentences, they then pass their paper to the right, and the second person reads the first person's sentences and writes the second sentence, beginning on a new line.

The second person should then fold the first person's sentence to the back so it's not visible. The second person passes to the next person, who can now see only one sentence. The third person writes their sentence on a new line, folds the paper again so only their sentence is visible, and passes it along.

This is repeated until it reaches the last person in the group, who is instructed to write a concluding sentence. The papers are passed back to the person who started it. Each person reads the paragraph to the group, and the group then votes on their favorite paragraph. The favorite is read aloud to the entire class.

EXAMPLE

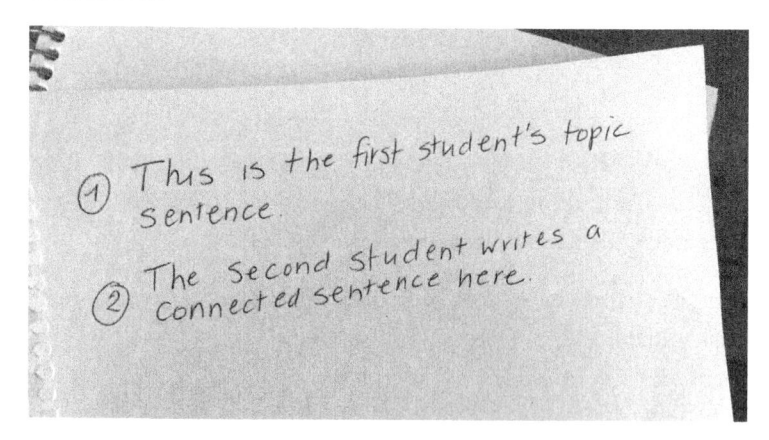

First step in the chain paragraph

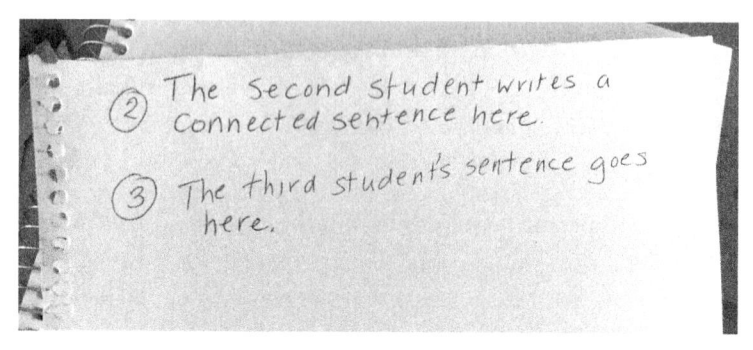

Second step in the chain paragraph; note the first sentence is now folded to the back and invisible.

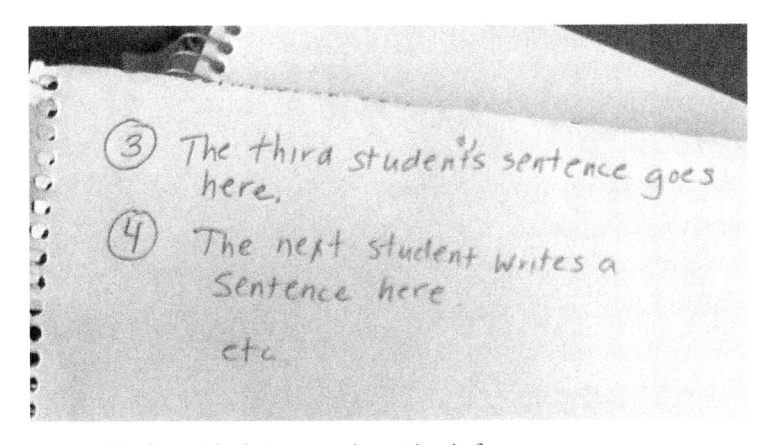

FIFTY WAYS TO TEACH WRITING

Third step in the chain paragraph; note that the first two sentences are now folded to the back and invisible.

20
FINISH THE STORY

This activity helps students make predictions and think about the order or stories. It is a good task when teaching organization skills in writing.

Find a level-appropriate story in a magazine, newspaper, or internet source. Remove the ending of the story.

Ask students to read the story (or read it to them). Next, ask them to imagine how it ends. They should write the ending they imagined. Students share their endings by reading them aloud or posting them on the wall.

End the activity by reading or sharing the original ending.

VARIATION

Do the same activity, but remove the middle or beginning of the story. Ask the students write the missing part.

21
"DEAR ABBY"

This activity is modeled after "Dear Abby," a newspaper advice column that was founded in 1956 by Pauline Phillips under the pen name "Abigail (Abby) Van Buren." It is written today by her daughter, Jeanne Phillips.

Find an advice column in a newspaper or on the internet (one in which people write to ask for advice on problems they are having in their personal lives), and copy out just the request for advice—not the response.

Ask students to write their response to the request. Ask students to share their answers and choose their favorites. If you want, share the published response to the problem with the class as well.

EXAMPLE

Here is a sample advice letter you might use:

Dear Wedding Advisor,

My wife's cousin got married last month. We are happy for her and her new husband. However, we weren't invited to the wedding! The whole family was invited, and even some distant relatives attended. But, not us.

We do not understand why we weren't invited. I thought of some reasons, but maybe you have an idea:

- Their guest list was too long, and they couldn't afford to invite us.
- They're mad at us. (But I don't know why.)
- They didn't want our children there, but they were embarrassed to tell us.
- They believed we couldn't pay to travel to the wedding, and didn't want to embarrass us.

I don't know what to do. Should I send them a wedding gift? Should I ignore them? What is your advice?

Sincerely,
Stayed at Home

22
MAP STORIES

This activity draws on students' memories of a location and focuses on storytelling.

Ask students to draw a rough map of their current neighborhood, or a neighborhood where they grew up. Have them locate a place on the map where an interesting story took place, and write that story[1].

VARIATION

Use an online map (such as Google Maps or Mapquest) and have students attach their stories to places on a collaborative map. See the article above for detailed instructions.

---

1. See the article "A Map to Communication: Google Maps," which I wrote about using maps in English Language Learning classes here: tesl-ej.org/pdf/ej59/int.pdf

23
DICTO-COMP

This is a variation on a dictation which has a long history.[1] This activity helps students to listen and interpret what they've heard, using their own words.

Instead of asking students to write exactly what they hear as in a standard a dictation, ask them to paraphrase, summarize, or expand upon a passage you read to them.

Choose a short passage with a strong main idea and read it to the class at least twice. Then, ask them to write about what they heard.

VARIATION

If you are working with lower-level students, write key words or phrases from the reading on the board and review them before the ditto-comp. This will help them complete their listening/writing task.

EXAMPLE

Here is a short passage that you can use to ask students to expand on the story:

> A new house is being built across the street from our school. There is a pile of bricks on the sidewalk in front of the new house. The bricks are stacked so badly that this pile blocks pedestrians from walking on the sidewalk. People who use wheelchairs cannot pass at all. We have decided to complain to the city about this problem.

---

1. See Paul Nation's article "Dictation, Dicto-Comp, and Related Techniques" at
    victoria.ac.nz/lals/about/staff/publications/paul-nation/1991-Dictation.

24
WRITE INSTRUCTIONS

This activity draws on students' knowledge, and helps them think and write about processes in organized ways.

Ask students to think about something they know how to do well—for example, cooking a dish, repairing a bicycle tire, tending a garden, etc. Have them write detailed instructions for this activity. Next, they should exchange their instructions with a partner and read each other's writing. They should ask each other questions about anything in the instructions that aren't clear. The original writer should revise accordingly.

Grammar note: Instructions should be written in the subjectless imperative form, such as *Stir the batter* or *Take the tire off of the rim*.

EXAMPLE

If you want to show your students a model of instructions, use a recipe from the internet, or use this one explaining how to defrost frozen food quickly without a microwave oven.

Step 1. Put your food in a leak-proof plastic bag.
Step 2. Place the bag in a large bowl.
Step 3. Fill the bowl with cold tap water.
Step 4. Leave the food in the cold water for 2-3 hours.
Step 5. Change the water out every 30 minutes to prevent it from warming.
Step 6. Take the food out of the bag and put it in a pan or in the oven to heat.

25

COMPARISON FOR RECOMMENDATION

This activity helps students develop the grammar and vocabulary for comparisons with the goal of making a recommendation.

Students should first identify two things that could be compared for the purpose of recommendation—for example, two different English classes, two current movies, two books to read, two local restaurants, etc.

As a pre-writing activity, have them list the pros and cons related to each option.

Finally, they follow up by writing a comparison essay, making a recommendation for one of their choices.

Movie 1		Movie 2	
Plus	Minus	Plus	Minus
My favorite actor	It starts really late	Gets good reviews	I don't know much about it

26

WRITE TWO LETTERS

This activity requires students to think about voice and tone in writing.

Have students imagine they do not have enough money for books or some other important expense in their daily life. They need to borrow a significant (but not huge) amount of money.

In order to borrow this money, they each write two letters. In the first letter, they should ask a close family member or good friend for a loan. In the second, they should ask a bank or financial institution for the money.

Before they write their letters, discuss what the requirements for each type of letter are: how a personal request is different from a formal request, for example.

After they have written their letters, show some good examples on the projector or in a handout.

27
INDEX CARD SUMMARIES

This gallery walk activity helps students summarize by limiting the amount of space they have to convey the main points of a reading.

After reading an article or short story, ask students to summarize what they read on one side of a single index card (3"x5" or 7.6 x 12.7 cm).

Pin the cards to a board or tape them on the walls around the room. Students should walk around the room and read all the summaries, taking notes on any differences they notice among the summaries.

Next, hold a class discussion about the differences they found in the summaries. Discuss which details seemed to be the most important.

Ask students to revise and rewrite their summaries after the discussion.

28

MOVIE AND BOOK REVIEWS

This activity helps students think critically about their reading or viewing. It can be done with a book students have read (or a movie viewed) for class, or as an independent activity.

Provide a model for the review from the internet or from a newspaper or magazine. Read the model reviews together as a class and discuss the major parts of them.

If students need models of reviews, for movies, rottentomatoes.com has a range of examples. For books, goodreads.com has a lot of user reviews.

Finally, have students write a review of either a book they've read or a movie they've seen recently. Encourage them to post their reviews on public sites, to become part of the 'conversation' about media.

Share the reviews in a student newsletter or on a website if you have one available.

29
BLANK COMICS

This activity helps students use their imagination to create dialogue.

Find a comic strip from a newspaper or online that you can print on paper. Using correction fluid, remove the dialogue from the original comic dialogue bubbles.

Copy the comic with the dialogue removed; ask students to write dialogue into the bubbles.

Share student comics by putting them on the wall or looking at them in groups.

One example is shown below. More photocopiable sample comics are found at anglofile.com/50ways. (Make sure you save comics that worked particularly well for use in future classes.)

Examples are found on the next pages.

MAGGIE SOKOLIK

Blank comic handout 1

FIFTY WAYS TO TEACH WRITING

Blank comic handout 2

Blank comic handout 3

30
ADVERTISEMENT

This activity is a good group project that encourages creativity and draws on students' prior knowledge of and exposure to advertising.

Students work in groups of three or four. As a group, they choose a product they want to advertise. The group designs and develops a written advertisement for that product, such as one that could appear in a magazine or newspaper.

They should add photographs (found in magazines or online) or drawings. It's a good idea to let students be creative with this. Encourage them to make attractive advertisements.

VARIATION

Students write a television or internet advertisement and act it out for the class or video-record it to share.

31
WHAT/WHO AM I?

This is a game-type activity that helps students develop their vocabulary and ability to describe objects or people. It provides useful practice in circumlocution.

Students write the numbers 1-5 down the left side of a sheet of paper. They then write ten clues for a person or thing that is known to other classmates.

Students then read their list of clues and others guess what is being described.

Grammar note: These should be written in first person: "I am..." or "We are...").

EXAMPLE

Clues for the objects "books," for example, might say:

1. We are long or short.
2. We use lots of words.
3. Sometimes we have pictures.
4. You have to use us in this class.
5. There are thousands of us in the library.

32
THESIS STATEMENTS

Students often find writing thesis statements for papers a difficult task. A lot of practice in both writing and evaluating thesis statements is necessary to master this skill.

To guide students through the process, ask them to start with a blank sheet of paper (or blank computer screen). Then, ask them to do these steps in order:

1. Students write the question they want to answer in their paper—either one you've given them or ones they have come up with on their own. This could be done in the form of a question or statement.
2. They write down the paper topic. These can be just a few words that generally describe the main topic.
3. Ask students to state their positions—that is, what do they believe to be true about the topic?
4. They next list any qualifications or exceptions to what they believe. That is, they think of disagreements others might have and list them. This could be in the form of a statement that begins *In spite of* or *Despite*.

5. They write down the reason they still believe their claims to be correct, even given the qualifications.

After they have completed these steps, they can practice putting all the information together into one or two sentences that clearly state what their essay will be about.

Have them put their draft thesis statements on the board. Other students should discuss whether their classmates' thesis statements are: clear, grammatical, arguable, provable, and interesting.

A photocopiable worksheet for developing thesis statements is found at anglofile.com/50ways, and is included here.

EXAMPLE

Thesis Statements

Think about your essay assignment. Write answers to these questions. An example of how to fill this page out follows.

Step 1: What question do you want to answer in your paper? Maybe it's one your instructor has given to you or one of your own.

Step 2: What is your paper topic? This can be just a few words that describe your main idea (it might help to think of this as your title).

Step 3: What is your position? That is, what do you believe to be true about your topic?

Step 4: What exceptions or counter-arguments are there to your ideas? That is, what disagreements might others have?

List them here. You might start your explanation with: In spite of or Despite.

Step 5: Why do you think you are right, even though some people might disagree? Think of all the information you have written about here.

Now, put it together in one or two sentences that will form your thesis statement.

~

Thesis Statement: Sample

Think about your essay assignment. Write answers to these questions. An example of how to fill this page out follows.

Step 1: What question do you want to answer in your paper? Maybe it's one your instructor has given to you or one of your own.

Should smoking be made illegal in all public places?

Step 2: What is your paper topic? This can be just a few words that describe your main idea (it might help to think of this as your title).

Smoking is bad for everyone: Make it illegal.

Step 3: What is your position? That is, what do you believe to be *true* about your topic?

I believe that smoking is unhealthy, not just for the people who smoke, but for the people around them. They also create a lot of litter by throwing cigarettes on the ground.

Step 4: What exceptions or counter-arguments are there to your ideas? That is, what disagreements might others have? List them here. You might start your explanation with: *In spite of* or *Despite*.

In spite of the fact that smoking is unhealthy, many people believe that it is their right to do what they want with their own health, and they believe smoking is enjoyable.

Step 5: Why do you think you are right, even though some people might disagree?

I believe that even though some people want their rights, other people have a right to breathe clean air and not see cigarette trash on the ground.

Think of all the information you have written about here. Now, put it together in one or two sentences that will form your thesis statement.

Although many people believe that smoking should be an individual choice, in fact, smoking harms people and should be made illegal in public places.

33
CRAZY PARAGRAPH

This activity helps students focus on using vocabulary in context.

Find a paragraph of the appropriate level for your students. Replace some of the main vocabulary items (nouns, verbs, adjectives, adverbs) with "silly" words of the same type.

Have students read the paragraph and locate the silly words, cross them out, and then write in more typical ones. Students can then share their rewritten paragraphs.

EXAMPLE

Original:

My friend Terry is a very nice person. She is always helping people. She visits sick friends and takes them soup, and she spends time reading to children at the library. She brings dinner to her neighbor because he cannot cook for himself. She takes her mother's dog for a walk because her mother uses a wheelchair. Terry is the kindest person I know.

79

With silly words:

My *car* Terry is a very nice *tree*. She is always *eating* people. She visits *short* friends and takes them *lamps*, and she spends time *reaching* to children at the *racetrack*. She brings dinner to her *laptop* because he cannot *jog* for himself. She takes her mother's *window* for a *movie* because her mother uses a wheelchair. Terry is the *fastest* person I know.

VARIATION

Do the reverse--give students the original paragraph and have them substitute silly words for some of the main vocabulary items. This will work best if you have completed this tip according to the original instructions first.

34
WRITE A PROPER EMAIL

This exercise is especially useful for students who may be looking for jobs, but may be helpful for any student who has to write email messages to anyone besides friends or family.

Ask students to write you an email as practice. First, students should write short but specific subject lines. Remind them that subject lines that say "hello!" or "information" do not tell the reader what the message is about.

Next, they should next include a proper salutation, including a correctly spelled name. The first sentence of the message should state the purpose of the email.

Then, no more than one paragraph should be written to explain the main point. They should sign with their full names after an appropriate closing.

Finally, they must proofread their messages for information and for grammar/spelling before sending them.

EXAMPLE

> Subject: University Research Position
>
> Dear Mr. Maler,
>
> I'm reaching out today because I am interested in the research position advertised on your website. I feel that my qualifications match the ones listed in your advertisement.
>
> I am attaching my résumé, which details my experience in this type of position.
>
> Please let me know if I can supply additional information. I look forward to hearing from you.
>
> Sincerely,
> Marina Gato

35
MODEL PARAGRAPHS

If your students are working on essays or other assignments that require well-formed paragraphs, it can be useful to supply them with models to analyze.

Use a projector or hand out models for discussion. Have them highlight topic sentences, support, transitions, and concluding statements. After discussing the parts of the paragraph, have them write their own paragraphs based on the models.

EXAMPLE

A good paragraph has a topic sentence, an explanation or example, and a concluding sentence that transitions to the next paragraph.

Look at this example.

The first statement tells us the main idea. →	The painkiller ibuprofen can be a fatal poison. People are used to taking ibuprofen when they feel pain, such as a headache. It is true that ibuprofen is an effective painkiller; however, ibuprofen, like any other medicine, can be harmful. Using too much of it may result into the damage to the stomach, liver, and heart. It is proven that excessive use of ibuprofen turns can cause many problems. Thus, the careful use of ibuprofen is advised so that it does not cause harm.
The next sentences give examples of the main idea.	
This paragraph ends by restating the main idea. This sentence could easily lead into a new paragraph about what careful use might mean.	

Now try it yourself with this topic sentence:

Topic sentence: Having pets is important, as it is shown they help you live a happier life.

(Give examples of the main idea here.)

_____

_____

_____

_____

(Write a concluding sentence here.)

_____

_____

Photocopiable sample paragraphs are found at anglofile.com/50ways.

36

USING TRANSITIONS

Students focus on the proper use of transitional markers in this activity. They will work in groups collaboratively to write a story using transitions appropriately. A good topic for the story is something that they did recently.

Start by giving students a list of transitions they might use in their stories. This chart presents some transitions, their purpose, and words associated with the concept.

Transition	Example word/phrase
Cause and effect	Therefore, as a result, so, consequently
Clarification	That is to say, in other words, to clarify
Contrast	But, however, on the other hand
Example	For example, for instance
Emphasis	Above all, most importantly, certainly
Enumeration	Firstly/secondly, further, and, moreover, in addition
Time	Meanwhile, during, subsequently, after that
Similarity	Likewise, similarly, in the same vein
Summarize/conclude	In conclusion, to sum up, in short

VARIATION

For advanced students, require them to use a specific number of transitions in their stories.

37
PARAPHRASE

Students sometimes struggle with paraphrasing because they rely too much on the original text, and use too much of the original language from it.

In this exercise, give students a short text to read—this could be on a single sheet of paper or projected on a screen. Give them enough time to read carefully.

Next, they should turn the printed page over so they can't see it (or you can blank the screen on the projector).

On a sheet of paper, the students should paraphrase what they just read. Let them consult the original once or twice, but only briefly.

They should compare their paraphrases in pairs or groups to see if they captured the main ideas accurately.

You should repeat this exercise frequently, as it's a skill that takes some time to master.

38
CULTURE WIKI

This activity is a collaborative, student-centered way for students to learn more about cultural references in their home or regional cultures. It requires that students have some internet skills and access.

Ask students to collaboratively create a wiki that explains important cultural elements of their own cultures, or of an English-speaking culture, such as Australia, Canada, or the U.S.A.

Students should identify cultural artifacts, such as festivals, gestures, etc., and create a dictionary-like entry explaining them.

Students can (and should!) edit each other's entries for correctness and completeness. This project can take place over several weeks or an entire school term.

Free wiki space is available in many locations online, including wikispaces.com (where you can find wikis for teachers as well).[1]

VARIATION

If you cannot or do not want to use the internet, this activity can be done on paper with students developing a glossary-style document.

---

1. You can learn more about wikis here: en.wikipedia.org/wiki/Wiki.

❦ 39 ❦
CREATE A CLOZE

This task helps students focus on writing vocabulary in context.

Find a passage and remove every fifth, sixth, or seventh word, replacing it with a blank line long enough for students to write an alternative word.

Ask students to fill out the cloze using words that fit the context.

An example cloze removing every fifth word follows.

VARIATIONS

1. Use examples of students' own writing to create the cloze activities
2. Instead of removing every fifth, sixth, or seventh word, remove every other noun, or just the pronouns, or whatever structure you want students to focus on.

EXAMPLE

The 2010 Winter Olympics, _____ known as the XXI _____ Winter Games and also _____ as Vancouver 2010, was _____ international winter sport event _____ was held in Vancouver, _____ Columbia, Canada. Some events _____ held in the surrounding _____ of West Vancouver and _____ the nearby resort town _____ Whistler. Approximately 2,600 athletes from 82 _____ participated in 86 events _____ fifteen disciplines. The 2010 _____ Olympics were the third _____ hosted by Canada and _____ first by the province _____ British Columbia. Canada hosted _____ 1976 Summer Olympics in _____, Quebec, and the 1988 _____ Olympics in Calgary, Alberta. _____ Vancouver is the largest _____ area to host the _____ Olympics, although Calgary is _____ largest city to host _____ Winter Olympics. They will _____ be surpassed by Beijing _____ 2022.

Solution:

The 2010 Winter Olympics, officially known as the XXI Olympic Winter Games and also known as Vancouver 2010, was an international winter sport event that was held in Vancouver, British Columbia, Canada. Some events were held in the surrounding suburbs of West Vancouver and in the nearby resort town of Whistler. Approximately 2,600 athletes from 82 nations participated in 86 events in fifteen disciplines. The 2010 Winter Olympics were the third Olympics hosted by Canada and the first by the province of British Columbia. Canada hosted the 1976 Summer Olympics in Montreal, Quebec, and the 1988 Winter Olympics in Calgary, Alberta. Metro Vancouver is the largest metropolitan area to host the Winter Olympics, although Calgary is the largest city to host the Winter Olympics. They will both be surpassed by Beijing in 2022.

40

SENTENCE COMPLETIONS

This activity helps students focus on sentence writing and subject-verb agreement .

Supply students with only the first or second half of five or ten sentences. Ask them to write the other part of the sentence. (Instead of creating and photocopying a handout, you could write the sentence prompts the board, and have students write the completions in their notebooks.)

EXAMPLES

Here are some sentence parts you could use:

1. Yesterday, I was really tired, so _____.
2. _____, so I went to bed early.
3. It's important to study regularly because _____.
4. _____ because you want to be prepared to do well on your final projects.

5. The water is really cold, so _____.

6. _____; therefore, I am going to buy a new book.

III
EDITING AND REVISING

Editing and revising are often confused for one another. Students, reading or listening to feedback on their writing, are often told they need to revise their work. However, what they sometimes do is edit it instead.

Revision is a "new look" at a piece of writing. It may mean reorganizing ideas, changing a thesis, supplying more support, or even starting over!

Editing, on the other hand, attends to the surface problems of a piece of writing: spelling, minor grammar errors, punctuation, and formatting.

Writing needs to be both revised and edited; however, revision should come first. There is no use in spending a lot of time in fixing the grammar and punctuation of a paragraph that is going to be eliminated altogether.

Students are sometimes hesitant to revise, and hope that editing will be enough. Encourage students to keep looking at their own work with fresh eyes. Also, encourage students to get others to look at their work and give honest feedback. Writing can always be improved through revision. Let students know it's a normal practice in writing, and that no one writes something perfectly the first time.

41
WRITER'S MEMO

A lot of dissatisfaction with feedback comes from student writers who expect comments on specific parts of their work, but the reader comments on a different aspect of it.

Before students turn in a writing assignment, ask them to write you a memo, in which they explain the following ideas:

1. What they are most proud of in their assignment
2. What they struggled most with
3. What comments they would like back from you

They should turn in their memo with their assignment.

Use their memos to guide your grading and commenting if possible.

VARIATION

If your students are job-oriented, require them to write the memo in proper business memo format.

42
WRITING ON THE WALL

Feedback from a variety of readers is usually helpful to student writers. This gallery walk activity is one way to have students give and get a lot of feedback on their writing.

Have students tape a recent rough draft of a writing assignment on the walls of the classroom. Post a blank piece of paper next to each assignment.

Students should then walk around the room and read their classmates' assignments, and then write comments about them on the blank paper. The comments could be about the grammar or vocabulary, the ideas and organization, creativity, etc.

When the activity is finished, the students gather their comments along with their assignments to help them revise and edit their writing with guidance from the comments.

43
REVERSE OUTLINING

You can help students understand how well they've organized their papers by teaching them to reverse outline.

Instead of having students write an outline before they begin their papers, have them outline a paper they have already finished.

They should read their papers through and write the main ideas in outline form. One approach is to tell them to read their papers paragraph by paragraph and write down the main idea of each paragraph first, and then fill in the supporting ideas.

This practice can help students see where their paper may lack organization, coherence, or clarity.

VARIATION

Have students read papers in pairs and outline each other's paper, following up with a discussion about parts that were unclear or unorganized.

44

KEEP AN ERROR JOURNAL

Students can make faster progress in their grammar understanding if they track their problems and start to notice patterns of error. One way to do this is by using error journals.

Using a set of returned assignments, students should track the type and number of errors that occur. They can do this in a notebook or a computer file.

They should note the date, the assignment, the type of error, example, and the number of times each error occurred in the assignment.

Next, they should include notes about how to fix the error, or anything discussed in class about it. Over time, they should see a decrease in the number of errors, or the types of errors.

Date	Assignment	Type of Error	Example	Number of times	Fix
Jan. 2, 2020	Comparison Essay	verb tense	Yesterday, I eat apples...	four	Do more exercises about verbs from the textbook.

Sample Error Journal Entry

45
SEARCH AND REPLACE

Sometimes, students are unaware of the editing tools that are available to them on their laptops or other devices. If students are using word-processing, it is a useful practice to be sure they know how to use the spelling and grammar checkers effectively.

Using word-processing software, students can also use the "search and replace" function to help them repair some common errors or writing weaknesses.

For example, if a student regularly writes *use to* instead of *used to*, he or she can put "use to" in the search box and see if this error appears in the assignment. By putting "used to" in the replace box, they can go through their papers and replace them where it's necessary.

Similarly, if students overuse a modifier like *very*, they can search for it automatically and evaluate whether it is a useful modifier in the context. Caution students not to automatically replace things without checking them carefully first!

46

ERROR CORRECTION IN CONTEXT

Grammar and writing books often present examples that look very different than the writing students produce. For that reason, it is helpful to use students' own writing to exemplify grammar or vocabulary points.

After students have submitted a draft essay or other writing assignment, anonymously choose one sentence from each student's assignment (or selection of assignments) that requires some editing or revision. The sentences should include different types of errors.

Copy the sentences onto a worksheet and make copies for the class or project them on the screen. Have students work in pairs to suggest corrections for each of the sentences.

Choose students to write the corrected sentences on the board and explain the corrections they made. Make further corrections if necessary.

47

DEMONSTRATE REVISION

Students sometimes don't understand the process of revision, believing it to be only a process of correcting spelling or word choice. The best way to help their understanding is to demonstrate the process in class.

Bring in a text that needs revision, preferably something that you have written or another fluent speaker (to make the point that even experienced writers revise their work).

Using a projector or document camera, revise the tex while talking about the decisions you are making about what to correct and how to change the text.

VARIATIONS

1. If you do not have a projector available, give students a 'before and after' version of a short document that has been revised, and discuss the changes that were made, and why.

2. Instead of explaining the revisions made, ask students if they can figure out why the revision choices were made. They can discuss this in small groups before presenting their answers.

❧ 48 ❦
PREPARE FOR PEER READING AND REVIEW

When peer review is unsuccessful, it is often because students have not been coached in effective ways to respond to each other's writing. Take time to discuss with students what makes for a good peer review–kindness, tact, focusing on information and clarity rather than grammar, or whatever points you want students to focus on in their reviews.

After the peer review training has been completed, in pairs or small groups, have students read and comment on each other's work. After work has been peer reviewed, students should also be given an opportunity to respond to the review, either to explain how the issues will be addressed, or to clarify any points of the writing. Here are some points you can use.

∽

Peer Review

Paper written by _____

Response by _____

1. Do you understand your partner's main point? Summarize it here. What can your partner do to improve it, if necessary?

_____
_____
_____
_____

2. Are there any parts that still aren't clear to you? Mark them on the paper, and explain them here.

_____
_____
_____
_____

3. What further work does your partner need to do before turning a final version in? Be specific.

_____
_____
_____
_____

After you finish this worksheet, give it to your partner and discuss your comments.

A photocopiable peer review worksheet is found at anglofile.com/50ways.

49
CHANGING NOUNS TO VERBS

A lot of weak writing comes from relying too much on nouns and some form of the verbs *be, do, have, give,* and *make,* rather than finding precise verbs that have the same meaning. Here are several common examples:

- *make a decision = decide*
- *have an argument with someone = argue*
- *take into consideration = consider*
- *give us information = inform*
- *do an analysis = analyze*
- *give approval = approve*
- *make an interpretation = interpret*
- *be in agreement = agree*

Ask students to find examples in their own writing, or supply them with examples from some of their assignments. Ask them to look for nouns or noun phrases that could be changed to verbs.

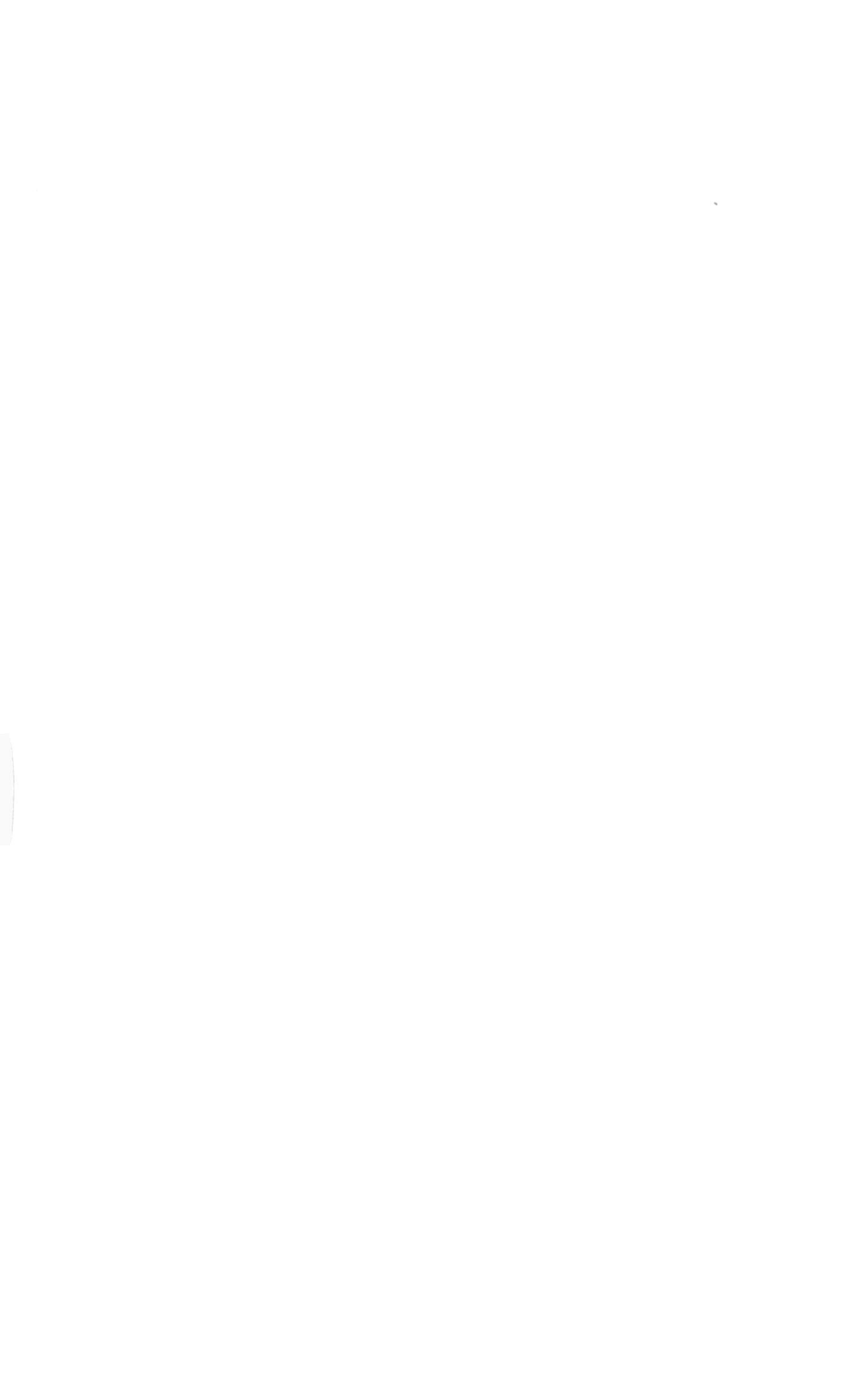

50

LISTEN TO YOUR WRITING

Students can sometimes hear problems with their writing that they overlook when reading, or even when reading aloud to themselves.

One solution to this is to have a computer read it to them. If students have Apple computers, they can copy the text of their writing into a TextEdit file (found in Utilities or Applications). If they have PCs, they may have a reader installed, or can download Natural Reader for free: naturalreaders.com. Online tools such as Google Translate (translate.google.com) can also read text aloud.

1. First, students print out a double-spaced copy of their paper. They need to have a pencil or highlighter.
2. Then, they listen to the computer read their papers as they follow along on the printed copy.
3. They stop the program when they hear a problem and note it on their paper.
4. They should listen especially for these types of problems: missing endings or subject-verb agreement

errors; ideas that don't fit together—for example, sentences that jump around or don't seem in the right place; repetition of words or simple repetitiveness; sentences that don't make sense; unnatural pauses, or lack of pauses, in the reading. This indicates incorrect punctuation; words the program can't pronounce, which could indicate a misspelling; wrong words.

BONUS TIP: STORY BOX

This activity helps students write clear and interesting sentences.

Use three colors of paper or index cards.

On pieces of one color, write nouns. On another color, write verbs. On the third color, write modifiers (adjectives or adverbs). You should have several of each color, each with different nouns, verbs, or modifiers (scale this according to your class size).

Put all of the papers or cards in a box. Ask a student to draw one of each color and read them aloud. Each student should then write a sentence using all of the words. Then, ask another student to do the same, continuing until all the cards are gone.

If you have a large class, prepare several sets, and let students work in large groups.

BONUS TIP: STORY BOX

VARIATION

Add more colors and categories; for example, put adjectives and adverbs in different categories, or separate one-word adverbs from prepositional phrases, such as *early* and *at 4:00 in the morning*.

Printed in Great Britain
by Amazon